THE TINY STORY BOOK

A picture book

G. W. HOBBS

[ZHINGOORA BOOKS]

LITTLE ALLIE.

I have been to see my little cousin Alice. She is just three years old, and I love her dearly. She has many things to play with. She has a ball, a rattle, and a horse; and she had a nice wax doll given her last Christmas, but as she got the paint off its face by kissing, it is laid by till she is bigger. We played she was my baby, and I dressed her up and took her to walk; after that we played have tea, and then I rocked her to sleep, and she looked so nice I could not help kissing her. She is coming to see me next week.

THE SHIP.

My brother Ben has gone to sea. He has gone in a big Ship. Mother packed his trunk with nice clothes, and put in his Bible and some good books, and I put in my picture, and we went to see him sail. I felt bad enough, for mother says he will be gone a whole year.

What a long time to be on the water! He says, when he comes home he will bring mother a nice shawl and me some fine playthings. I hope he will not get lost at sea, as some poor sailors have been.

THE DEAD ROBIN.

See, Charles, how little Robin lies:The film is on
his gentle eyes;His pretty beak is parted
wide,And blood is flowing from his side.

And Willy, when from school he comes,Will run
and get some little crumbs,And fling them
round, and wait to seeRobin hop lightly from the
tree,

To pick the crumbs up, one by one,And sing
and chirp, when he has done;—Then when I
show him Robin dead,How many bitter tears
he'll shed!

THE RIDE.

This little girl is having a ride. She has a nice carriage, and a pretty goat for a horse. I think her brother must be very kind to her. I had a ride in a goat carriage once; it was on Boston Common; father put little Arthur and me into the carriage, and we rode along, holding the reins, as happy as could be. After the ride was over, we went to the Public Garden and fed the ducks and fishes, and then we had a sail in the boat. I hope we shall go again next summer.

THE LION.

Let me tell you a short story about a Lion. Once a poor Negro found that a Lion was following him, as he was walking along through the woods. The Lion was watching for a chance to spring upon him. The man was very much frightened, but walked swiftly along till he came to a very steep bank; here he quickly placed his hat and cloak on a bush, to make it look like a man, and then he crept away. The Lion, thinking it was the man, was silly enough to spring upon the cloak, and tumbled on the rocks below.

LEARNING TO READ.

Come, little brother, come to me;I'll teach you
soon your A, B, C.You're three years old; you
must, indeed,Begin at once to learn to read.

Be careful now, don't tear the book,And where I
point there you must look.That's A, that's B, and
that is C;Now say them plainly after me.

That's very well! How very nice!You'll learn your
letters in a trice.And then you'll quickly learn to
spell,And soon, I hope, read very well.

GETTING UP.

Baby, baby,Ope your eye,For the sunIs in the sky;

And he's peeping once again,Through the frosty window pane.Little baby, do not keepAny longer fast asleep.

There, now, sit in mother's lap,That she may untie your cap;For the little strings have gotTwisted into such a knot!

SUSY BROWN.

Susy Brown is a good girl; she is willing to give up her play, and stay at home to take care of the baby. Some of her friends were going to the woods and fields to pick berries, and Susy wanted to go with them; but when she came home from school, and found her mother tired and worn with her work and the heat, Susy took the baby and said she would stay at home and let her mother rest. When the girls came home with their berries, they all gave Susy some, for every body loves Susy.

THE SQUIRREL-TRAP.

Henry had seen a squirrel in a cage; he had watched him whirling about and cracking his nuts, and he longed to have one of his own; so he built a trap-cage, and set it near the great nut tree. He set it in the morning, and then went to school, but he could not study much for thinking of the trap. After school it did not take him long to visit the old nut tree, and lo! there was a little squirrel in his trap; but little squirry soon got away, as you see, and ran off to the woods, happy enough to get his liberty again.

THE SQUIRREL.

One pleasant summer morningA little boy was
seenBeneath a spreading oak treeUpon a
village green.

And to a merry squirrelThe child was heard to
say—"How is it, Mr. Muncher,You always are at
play?"

"I laid up nuts, last autumn,So I can frolic
now,"Replied the merry squirrel,And frisked
along the bough.

"And you, my little school-boy,Must study all you can,And lay up stores of knowledge,To use when you're a man."

Near by a bird was stoppingTo rest its pretty wing—"Pray, tell me," said the youngster,"Who taught you how to sing?"

"I never had a master,"The little bird replied;"But when my mate was sitting,To comfort her I tried;

"And if you like my singing,Its secret I will tell—
All that we do for love, sir,We surely shall do
well."

And now, dear little children,If you open wide
your eyes,You will see the pretty lessonsIn
creatures, birds, and skies.

How doth the little busy beeImprove each shining hour,And gather honey all the dayFrom every opening flower!

In books, or work, or healthful play,Let my first years be passed,That I may give for every daySome good account at last.

THE SWING.

"Oh! is it not a nice swing!" said Amy to her little brother; "how cool it makes you to swing in the shade! I love papa for fixing this swing, don't you? We will kiss him when he comes home."

Amy loves to swing her little brother better than to swing herself; but sometimes she swings, and holds little Eddie in her lap. What nice times little children have, when they love each other, and try to please!

THE POOR BEGGAR.

"Mother, I am so hungry," said Charley Gray, as he returned from school. "Why!" said his mother, "did you not eat the dinner that you carried with you?" "No, dear mother; as I was going to school, I saw, sitting by the roadside, a poor old man and a little girl; they looked so sad and tired that I stopped to speak to them; they said they were very hungry—so I gave them my dinner, and went without myself. I am glad I did it, for it must be dreadful to suffer from hunger."

THE DIRTY BOY.

Here is a poor boy; he is going to have a wash at the pump. His clothes are all torn and soiled, but he can keep his face clean, and he will soon be old enough to earn some better clothes.

Some little boys who have good clothes, and kind parents to keep them clean, hate to be washed. I have heard of a boy who had to be hired to have his face washed, and he would often cry about it, as though it was a dreadful thing. Children, to be loved, should be nice and clean.

SUMMER TIME.

I love to hear the little birdsThat carol on the trees;I love the gentle murmuring stream,I love the evening breeze.

I love to think of Him who madeThese pleasant things for me;Who gave me life, and health, and strength,And eyes, that I might see.

I love the holy Sabbath-day,So peaceful, calm, and still;And O! I love to go to church,And learn my Maker's will.

End of the book.

www.ingramcontent.com/pod-product-compliance
Lightning Source LLC
Chambersburg PA
CBHW060020300526
45794CB00003B/1228